Dreaming of Floods

Dreaming of Floods

Poems by
Stuart Friebert

Vanderbilt
University
Press
Nashville
1969

The author acknowledges with thanks the Oberlin College research status appointment that enabled him to complete this book.

Published in 1969 by Vanderbilt University Press, Nashville, Tennessee

The author and publisher make grateful acknowledgment to the editors of the following periodicals for permission to reprint those poems in this collection that first appeared in their periodicals and to Günter Eich for permission to publish the translation of "Gemischte Route."

The Activist: "The End" (Vol. VI, 1965); "In a lime tree on the French coast, celebrating not having been killed in the Invasion twenty years ago" (Vol. VI, 1966); "Small Town Fourth" (Vol. VII, 1966). *Arizona Quarterly:* "Kite Flying in Japan" (Vol. XXI, 1965). *Arts in Society:* "My Parents, My Life" (Vol. IV, 1967). *Border:* "Flying the Hypotenuse" (under title of "Inequality"); (Vol. I, 1965). *Cape Rock Quarterly: "Virginia Woolf* Premieres in our Neighborhood" (Vol. IV, 1966). *The Catholic World:* "Hunting with my Son" (under title "Young Hunter"); (Vol. 202, 1965); "Fishing off France, Summer 1945" (Vol. 205, 1967). *Descant:* "Poet in a Small Town" (Vol. X, 1966); "Shallow and Deep" (Vol. IX, 1965). *Dust:* "Taking the Express to Paris, Texas" (Vol. II, 1965). *Folio:* "Winter in Early Massachusetts"; "The Owl and the Pussy Cat" (Vol. II, 1966); "For the Morning" (under title of "Libation"); "Dinner with my Father, High Lake, Summer 1968" (Vol. IV, 1968). *Goliards:* "Wings and Circles" (Vol. II, 1965). *The Goodly Co:* "March 14, 1864"; "My Life Is Insane"; "To Watch It Snow" (Editor's Choice Award); (Vol. II, 1965). *Hiram Poetry Review:* "I Die"; "The House" (with a different final stanza) (Vol. II, 1967). *kayak:* "The Gunners" (under title "Above & Below"); "The Picture"; "Homing" (with a different final stanza); (Vol. X, 1967). *Mad River Review:* "From the Beginning" (Vol. II, 1966). *Michigan Quarterly Review:* "July 12" (under title "Vacation"); (Vol. IV, 1965); "Lake Mendota, Summer without You" (Vol. V, 1966); "In This House" (under title "Crossing the Heart"); (Vol. VIII, 1969). *Minnesota Review:* "Virginia Woolf's Diaries" (Vol. VI, 1966). *Podium:* "In the Mind's Eye"; "November" (Vol. I, 1965). *Poetry Northwest:* "The Winter of 1856" (Vol. VI, 1965); "On Jumping off the Queen Elizabeth in Summer" (Vol. X, 1969). *Prairie Schooner:* "Vietnam" (Vol. XLIII, 1969). *Quarterly Review of Literature:* "Dreaming of Floods"; "To the Statue of an Egyptian Queen in Rome"; "Last Visit"; "The Gift" (Vol. XIV, 1966). *Red Clay Reader:* "Honeymoon, Lake Gogebic" (Vol. IV, 1967). *The Smith:* "Old Graves"; "Ceremony for Churchill, St. Stephen's, Vienna" (Vol. II, 1965); "Ohio, 1965, England, 1940" (Vol. II, 1966); "Century after Century" (Vol. III, 1968). *The South Dakota Review:* "The Country Preacher" (Vol. II, 1964); "Source" (Vol. III, 1965). *South & West:* "Ballad of a Chinese Painter" (Vol. IV, 1965). *Trace:* "Dead Cat" (Vol. VI, 1965); "I always cut through, drop my hook . . ." (Vol. X, 1967); "My mother dies in Wisconsin while I am excavating in Egypt" (Vol. XIII, 1969).

Standard Book Number 8265–1141–4
Library of Congress Catalogue Card Number 72–88187
Printed in the United States of America by
Heritage Printers, Inc., Charlotte, N. C.

Contents

IV   Silent movies

V   It's me who hears the fountains

VI   The Middle-West Mystery

DIANE

I

West
to
East

Taking the Express to Paris, Texas

The hills wore morning butterflies,
transforming flight. Streams
smelled of wind in the mind.
The sun could rise no higher
and no farther could I fall.

Thoughts ripened, roots
deeper than chokecherry,
near water where dumb fish
spawn in a whirl
of bladeless knives.

Thoughts darken into larks
shredding the butterflies.
Candles come to the branches:
sunlight is sun and light.
The heart sinks deep,

cockles exploding undermind,
bottoms up. The mellow boat's
boards float in the foam. Those
blown sails will never be recovered
in the wind of the prairies.

The Country Preacher

He walked with the weather,
the Bible in the pale meadow of his hand,
preaching to homesteaders, looking at Indians
through their fires watching his eyes
like the roots of a medicine man.

The snake was out of breath, turned
its linen blue eyes at him, a vision
from the Atlantic to the Pacific noon,
reading verses into the snow and sand.

The snake's eye echoed more light
than the reeds or rocks. In the berry bogs,
it went farther ahead, binding him
in the Canaan twilight of its depth.

The Winter of 1856

The longest of any modern winter.
Snow on a level with you then suddenly
thirty feet deep in the ravines.

Elizabeth boarded some woodchoppers.
All the water she used washing after them
was snow, melted in boilers on the catalogue stove.

She remembered some deer
coming through clogged woods.
They walked into the sharp sun.

The men saw them. The deer
broke the color of the crust
and went too deep.

The woodchoppers,
shoeing the snow,
went for their axes.

March 14, 1864

Across the valley rotten with summer
the indolent armies wait while
Jackson rides to drink with Lee.

Trees are insects in the orchards.
Two officers stage a race
between Blues and Grays
cheering jumped ditches.

The recruits
pile fench rails and brush
on the swollen carcasses of horses.

Winter in Early Massachusetts

Thoreau awakened
from his lethargy
to the green dust on the walls
of his storehouse for roots and beans
and spent the days
deliberately.

The sun dusted the icy pond
as he tramped nine miles
through the vertical snow
to keep an appointment
with a yellow birch.

Harpooning the True Sunfish

I

Must not be confused
with the common shark.
Kills three times its weight,
loitering and providing.
Its eyes like a king's
float with dexterity.
Sleeps on its large,
exact, blue backbone.
Basks easily off
a foreign country.

II

Slide the thimble
between socket and ring.
Set the hook, the bone will
snap as simple as that.
It dives fairly deep
to die in two days.
Death washes off,
the carcass bobs up.
Turns a white belly
up to the sun.

III

Some kind of rash
breaks the skin.
The harpoon is still there,
its own property.
The sun goes for the liver,
it covers itself with instinct.

The Ceremony

Up north, under
the waves of Hudson Bay,
the fish suck the sap
from the bows and arrows
they used to use.

While they bragged,
priests from the south built
roads to the interior for
the frantic march and sent
for a son, born on ice.

He was weak and beggarly
but had good white teeth
the Eskimos prayed would
make good hooks for the trip
up and down the New Testament.

On windy days, reading worked,
love worked, on a calm day
they harpooned him
in the back. (I trust you
will finish the work I began?)

They washed his hair in urine,
made unusually sharp hooks
from his bones. At night, the
elders crossed the glacier, slept
with polar bears and left

no sons. O Christ,
memory of ruminal life, of
fishbeaks in the unfinished dark,
still snapping.

Ceremony for Churchill

St. Stephen's, Vienna

In the public garden, I sleep till
the bells rot through the cathedral's
walls. Drunks are scattered about the
frozen roses like broken furniture.
One from Hungary in a fedora
died toward morning.

Then the music comes
from the passing bassoons and oboes.
A Russian gunboat touches the little
white breasts of the Danube.
Men bend between pews, crawl
across the sermon on their knees
and kiss Churchill's flesh lying
several thousand miles away under
another rose, rose window.

I see both windows from my rosebed now,
wash the pigeon smear from my cheek
and walk marked by the guards
into the cathedral as though through
a mountain pass where one
can only look ahead.

Kite Flying in Japan

Cunningly rigged,
a square, circle, hexagon,
star, fish, dragon, man,
horse, shield, all
will fly equally well.

Whole families circus the air,
even crying children and animals
with hands and legs spread thin.

And old men, at night,
retired from life,
fly the loose skies,
lights on their tails
like giant ancestors.

To Russia, Summer 1968

for John Hobbs

The moon is done for, I
set out for Russia, spitting
on myself and pounding on others.

The heat in Kiev is virtuous
like a bus in the sun.
The streets wait for

a few odd scraps of people.
In my afternoon hotel room
the samovar is pale and the tea

furiously bright. The cakes
taste of little bits of metal.
After another meeting with

the lantern-jawed lady guide,
I am allowed to meet Kiev's
only woman poet. She comes

to the party dressed in
barbed wire and shows me a gun
at 11 pm. We sleep badly together

but meet for breakfast. The waiter
is a difficult, depressed Ukrainian.
He gives us limited instructions

for a drive to the river.
The old way of making the trip, as
a guidebook tells it in installments,

leads to water where birds
feed on black flora, leads
to a great many meetings with God.

II

Invasions

Driving a Gravel Road along the Danube

I stop the car to wave
at the weary young girls.
The straw air is heaped
all around us. For

a moment, they are
rather beautiful, matted
and holding to the ancient
faith, the hot August

morning ringing overhead.
The handles of their scythes
crack in their grip, their
tongues slip forward,

greedily. They break into
pieces when I take them
into my eyes, like small
failures. I look up to

the cutting moon.
It is working
like the ones in
old Dürer prints.

Virginia Woolf's Diaries

in memory of Addison Ward

The hay on the marshes near London
buries the falling light.
Should she think
of death?

A moth steers like a Messerschmitt
shot down on Sunday over the town,
the powder on its wings scrambling.

She walks along the bomb craters,
where birds nest. Moths and birds,
she can't stop looking till the
moon comes up like an owl, hooting.

I want to look back at her war,
the lovely free autumn fall
of the fire bombs, belonging.

Ohio, 1965, England, 1940

I drive across the macadam road past
the last Sohio station. Making certain
it is the right road is an enormous
relief. Bursts of sun scatter water

on the tar. There's a throbbing at the
back of my neck as all the lights of
London squish and sink, the rear view
mirror finally dulled by distance.

Something glistens over the county air-
port. It seems risky to cross the marsh
to the hangar. A plane like a worm hangs
in my brain. It's the enemy, I look high,

see more planes and the English insignia.
They slip and slide on the icy air. (This
afternoon I'll fly with my family to
quieter air) The pilot of the Cessna is

dressed in gray and a rough tie. Before
we take off, he drinks only one ounce
of scotch. My wife would have admired him
for that. The sun shines on the cock

swaggering with weather. Would you mind
if I took off? A hand to hand salute and
we climb gravely to our top altitude, then
coast slowly down over the smouldering

houses, mirrors still swinging in the ruins.
Who lives there? I suppose wife and child.
I used to listen for the church bells with
them, preferring one dead to both. Sorry

to break into your private life but the
twenty minues is up. (Tomorrow I shall go
to all the movies in town) The bombs explode
later and I pick bouquets from my still life.

17

The German Plans and the Chickens

In the center of the great hen house
the sky whirls, icons come to life
like hens on rafters, using their eyes
maliciously. Let me see the eggs, a
guard says, this is no time to be timid.
One by faultless one he turns them over,
piles them sheepishly high, stops the spin
of the yolks (was that life?). Another
guard breaks the ranks, holds his fingers
up like a rooster, clucks with his powerful
cheeks. The eggs admit defeat, accept
the German plans, lie down in the
incubator, heave and crack the air, begin
to worship the new god who is a celebrity,
turns out a thousand lives, grainy white,
just as obstinate now as before conception.
The barracks light goes out, trim German
shepherds lie down on purpose, the guards sleep.

Gemischte Route

(translation of "Gemischte Route"
by Günter Eich)

Finally the doors are locked,
the gas cocks turned to zero,
ashes in the oven, otherwise
no remains. We can go.

Nothing but ravines, tongues
of snow, where are the roses
of the teacher, the rain animals
through shattered windows, movie
programs through letter slots,
thursdays.

Where are, after tongues of snow,
after thursdays, our roads? Waldein
to Hiroshima, between dogs the
stairs in a quarry, a stretch
of comfort drawn from barracks,
from rotting grass, rotting ropes.

For the Morning

The guards
bring clean firewood,
opposing the tree, making
fire of the fat of the brain.
There is no pressure
to end the sacrifice.

The children
like tassels worn by old Jews,
gather at the well, hailing
God as some great friend, pulling
up milk for the morning.

In a lime tree on the French coast, celebrating
not having been killed in the Invasion twenty years ago

My mind goes to the edge of the branch
to cool off, memories like seaweed
come up foul and damp below. The space
between is as empty as the one between

dying soldiers. The wind blowing close
to the surface drags their faces
for a moment, the white mollusks
of their eyes, a vein swelling

in the center, float on the flat
waste of water or sink like shells
lost in the white wind of the current.
Twenty years later, from this crooked

lime tree, I see the fires they have
melted in the sand. The dumb crabs
will breed in the mud, waiting
for cooler weather. I am waiting

for the slow alphabet of heroes
to slide off the hunchbacked ice. I
wish I were these memories, my eyes
lie down on the white fur of the branches,

sleep slowly like sea balancing wrecked clouds.

Fishing off France
Summer 1945

Burly clouds
turn their wheel
into the Channel.

In the red foam
I cast under overcast
for the bodies

I know are there.
Night sweeps
toward the sand

and sits on boggy thrones.
My bait floats out of the weeds,
gleaming faintly.

Vietnam

I
22 hrs. from Kentucky
a varied flight
along the Pacific
past small
and large volcanoes.

A doctor from Mississippi
hunts wild geese in
his free time and talks so
there're almost no
misunderstandings.

With his womanshead
he goes after
the wet birds,
his gun's
in a good mood.

The birds
don't fly up, a
black head disappears
between two reeds.
There are smells.

II
In the bamboo
we walk for just
a short time.
Stanley and Henry
are our master sergeants.

The landscape on hill 822
is smoky, legs
snort like pinkish frogs.
For a moment
the crotch aches.

At one o'clock
we lie down
with our jaundice
while the rain
stumbles into the trench.

III
Through bacon trees
our unit sweats
a lot, later the
water goes back to
the pores like ground.

A bad moon. Birches
poke us like so much
horizon. The window
of the smallest tree
has confided in the enemy.

The Gunners

The gunners pump bullets
into the wings of the Starfighters.
Their ghosts gambol back
to the carrier. Everywhere,
the dust spreads, men
speak in statistics.

Off China,
in the flaking air,
a helicopter whispers I'll save you
to a pilot's head singing
to itself. His heart
floats off in a bottle
toward San Francisco. He lands
in an awful forest
where he must learn to be gentle. Above,
the stars peel off, leaving the moon
on fire in a ruined sky. Below,
red lobster shells litter the shore.

III

In
a
small
town

Lake Mendota, Summer without You

I step over the flat black ants
down to the water. My eyes rock
on the swimming women, slam into
the pier of unexpected desire.

The noise on their blue lips
is caught in the soft net of jazz.
(The lifeguard is not afraid
to play his guitar)

How can it be August, days
filtering through the mesh air?
I sit at a metal table, fanned
orange by the back of a chair

and serve myself cheap beer, turn
pages past modern German poetry,
light a Dutch cigar and believe
I shall never see you again

stripped like the sail of summer
out of time. My thoughts are
paper ships on the Asian table.
Slowly you sail out of mind.

Honeymoon, Lake Gogebic

I reach for my hip boots and hurry
to the edge of the pier. Over
red nets and old oars. The dawn
is beside me in a bronze bowl.
It dances out to meet the sun.
I tap at the water, a loon
comes up and lays a little yell
between the waves. We float
close for a while, dreaming.

A surge of blue
drowns me in a tide of petals.
(The flower in the hand of a virgin
is precise) At noon I search
the deep foamy sun. (All legends
belong to the virgin)

On the fourteenth day
we shake our rings into
seven feet of water. My wife cries
when I refuse to dive for them.
I am somewhere else. My
parents are there, warm
under the ice of our years
apart. They are not certain
how close they can approach
ice without its giving way.
I lie frozen, so the warmth
of my face surprises them.

They touch my hair, but I am
not at home. For a moment
they cling to the rim of my
eyes, holes slanting down to
snakes hurting from winter.
My father fires a gun at
the rolls of rattlers.

Bullets ricochet off the rocky
ledges in my mind. My children
peek out, a moon for a father
cradled in their arms. Their
heads float off to cry. Friends
are there grieving, the way cows
walk to keep warm in winter.

Rivers in spring will roll and
chase them away in good spirits.
Outside, the buildings are in
good repair. The wire fences I
have stretched all the way to
the water will keep the kids from
falling in. My black river body,

elongated, fills with white ice. It
is likely to outlast the winter.
My wife like a squaw guards me
till the moon of death passes,
the elms pop open with thaw,
squirrels curling in the holes.
On a limb they would crack, tied

to a crudely carved branch, I
shall sway till I'm as dark
as dry bones. From this Indian
burial, I thrust my limbs in
another direction, walk to stay
wild, cover myself with leaves,
kill a wife or a stranger.

Poet in a Small Town

Some throng the world, nailing coins to counters,
throwing toothbrushes away eventually, ultimately
outrunning the endless swells of hills writhing
with shadows. Me, I cannot run if I cannot fly
to alien lakes where hunters hide in bays, their
bullets skimming ducks that do not laugh. I am
tired of watching shadows climb from heart to eye.

Others plow past farms while this sad little town
wraps languor around my brain. Moved by sun and
rain, the fields yield a quick harvest. I loiter
at noon in camps of mute men, the country around
us waits. We play cards after lunch, smile and
die a while. Then I am alone in the shiny wheat
waiting for the church bells to sound like water

over wheat. It's time to move eyes, sniff for
bones or beer. There have been times when memory
was a shallow garden, the sun brooding over the
flowers. I found a quiet way through the flood
of light, charged the center of the act, lunged
for the bleeding I could not see. I know I was
teasing myself with sacrifice. Calm as the Egyptian

statues in the college museum, I am a future which
holds no past, bend to see the snake's eye fill
with fluid, run as I once ran to my wife washing
dishes at the kitchen window, leaves falling on the
dead birds of her hat. The vision gone,
she passes me now in the vexed stir within the walls.
I watch the gates of Ilium blur but fall.

The House

The Basement

There's a whole cow
in the freezer. The futility
of it, my God, what a
thing to happen.

The Kitchen

The determination
of my wife cooking
awes me. Our
married life smoulders.

The Dining Room

We make all the
necessary changes
while
eating.

The Living Room

Yes, we have been
successful. In
intimate groups we
discuss it.

The Children's Bedroom

In their beds, the wind
makes their hearts sail.
The bridge is impassable.
Who's touching them?

The Bathroom

Our daughter waves goodbye
to her BM. In the mirror
I see Dr. Spock. He
is smiling too.

The Master Bedroom

The cold glows
between the sheets. My
giddy wife pleads
for my electric penis.

The Attic

The ping pong ball
gets lost. We find
it in the electric
light socket.

Small Town Fourth

Our July blood whistles in the dust.
We stamp out the last popcorn buds,
our red hearts set for home.
All the children in town
flop out of the dark
like baby eagles. They
fly home on their own somehow.
Later they have spoiled dreams
while we take our wives to the floor.
Hail the Reverend! He doesn't
believe our kids like Sunday school, knows
we love the gusty Christian morning
but show no life.
Summer love hangs like Christ on the gallows.
He heads toward us nonetheless, the
last leaden flicker in his eyes (a
sky interfered with) disappears.

The key's lost,
I give my wife a friendly swat,
crash a window and wash the blood
away with one more beer.
Upstairs she flushes the toilet twice
and the clumsy cavalry chases Blue Indians
through the early movie. My organs
float up like a smoke signal
from Geronimo to White Doe.
What's left of our love
toils like a last cloud
through the rancid American air.

Homing

I pray on the train, a church
of speed. Opposite my words
it is snowing. Under my tongue
birds fly to a southern wedding.
Desire   fades   to a letter.

But the train damages the snow.
Trees pop up in yards, exclaiming!
Near the last tunnel, weeks
of broken water eat at the wall.

In the morning, my wife hurries
downstairs. I pay her all possible
attention and get the best of the
breakfast. There's no lull before
she and I grit eyes to eat. To eat.

Hunting with my Son

The mallards fly
with moss on their foreheads.
They fly across the stubble
of last year's cattails
stretched out over the open water.

My son enjoys
the recoil of his 12-gauge,
watches the white smoke
of our guns barking
from the marshes, the moon
in his eyes falling
heavy and slow
into a white nest.

Virginia Woolf Premieres in our Neighborhood

I wake up face down, feel
the movie of another morning
on my shoulders and laugh.

"You don't play my games,"
Diane says, up all night
thinking that.

Forget those childish things,
I say in my dark mouth. Soon
her head detaches itself

like a balloon
cut free
floating over me.

For the last time, she runs
my bath (her eyes like Taylor's
turning back toward some soft beach)

(for the first time I think
she is not a child)
and drowns my beached voice.

I always cut through, drop my hook . . .

The snow hustles over the runners
of the porched sleds or your heavy
thighs or howls like a lost virgin
getting it from a first-rate devil.
The cat bends over the cold, ice
pods snapping on her bushy legs.
She smells the semen coming long

before you see the car lights, greets
me looking right at my crotch. (I
want to run the cat down) You're
only flirting again, the sun stretches
on the branch of your kiss. The kids
radiate hope through the furry windows.
They don't need a father any more so

let's love out here, strict like ice.
(You always turn from time to time
to check the surface of your lust)
I always cut through, drop my hook
and pull you up. Your mouth turns
with speed and anger
into a flying fish.

The End

It is the end of the year.
One more like it between me and my students
and everything will be over.
The grants have all fallen through.
Friends kiss theirs and drive off
before dawn for Volvograd or Athens,
their hairy arms hanging from new sleeves.
Guards in grass-green uniforms
let them pass borders but pinch their wives,
extremely tall, who glitter in the fog.
Some townspeople leave for Cleveland.
The Greyhound bench is splintered
so they stand and smoke and stare.
I stare back through beige drapes
so hot the air-conditioning stops
and my head falls on a clean desk
and dies a while. My ears hear
the cheers of a hundred thousand tourists.
In several places at once
military bands warm the frozen anthem.
My favorite student wakes me with a cheap cigar,
still bringing it to her father, hating him.
(I must teach her to feel them for freshness)
She stays on the whole summer, consoling me,
painting, exploring sex.
I hold up my pencil to my eyes, measuring.
This town is full of girls
smelling of their 5 and 10, legs too thin
to wake the Blacks sitting against the drugstore
on a ledge so thin it must slit their asses.
Some women pass back and forth
between butcher shop bargains.
I hurry out to protest the price
of hamburger, flush and withdraw
bundles of words I have tied all
my life. At home, my wife paints

and cooks and has children. I
get a meal like a still life
and wish I could burp like my son
or be hung like my wife's paintings.
She walks around like the Day of
Atonement, "Don't worry honey, you'll
have time." I don't have time. I've
been to Zürich where Joyce and Trotsky
ordered apricot brandy from the
ruthless waiters of the Odeon Cafe.
They always got drunk by early evening.
In the early evening, my wife and I
go to the failing Summer Theater.
The long comedy isn't funny.
"What sort of husband will he make?"
"You'll starve with him, you'll starve for nothing."

IV

Silent
movies

Wings and Circles

I lie without life,
die without flesh,

like the feet of mallards
soft and blind.

My body wants the place
where wings and circles are.

The Picture

My father sniffs
at the road, the fine sand
stones, yells his cows across
the wooden river, the wheels
of the wagon all sounding different.

He doesn't mind
looking at the ducks
jailed in the reeds. Farther on
the church and mill grow dark
before he passes.

Then he simply arrives,
we call out in curly voices
from the porch, offering our youth
growing in rain. It is not
his fault, he can not

see us, lined up, waiting.
Casually he moves from me to
my brother, watching the sin
in the background. We have always
been afraid to develop the picture.

Dinner with my Father
High Lake, Summer 1966

My father gallops to the ends of bays, sipping
the essence of the water's genitalia, rinsing
his mouth with a hub of things, ultimately catching
the fat, sweet loon off guard. It drops its

call in a pledge of good faith. The sound is
very long and goes up and down the furrows. My father
dries the blood quickly in the rough water, imbeds
the gravid head in the small intestine. The feet

presumably die and are cut off for sauce. The anus
opens slowly, out drop a lot of lime balls into the
interprismatic spaces of water. Far below damp
seaweed traps them in great numbers. In the icehouse

the body is identified, weighed, sexed and measured,
bilious organs removed and put in warm saline solution.
One single yellow egg pops from the uterus, it is
clearly in the 8 cell stage, still getting instructions

from the thirsty darkness. We sit down gravely
near the carcass, my father carves and speaks in
arched curves covered with worms. They forage and
the infection spreads to the mainland.

My Father Dies Drowning

The dried branches of the poplars
flare up, my father is out of breath.
He dives up but shoots back down
with a large black fish and dies.

Cry naturally, silently
at proper moments as the words
of the priest slide like diamonds
down my throat. Gradually,

my mother fills bellies of trout
for our Russian relatives. They
distend with silver gifts which
she saves for the first anniversary.

I reach down like rust
to touch the small green moon nesting
in my father's shoulder. Fish
swim through his eyes gently.

I must clean those fish now but
wash away around the cool bend
of memory, the fish dying like
songs of wind, the relatives sitting

and sipping from the jug of summer.
My father's smile fights but falls
back into the water where I bury
the fish-bone skeleton of his heart.

In This House

On the table, the old Bible
flaps its wings like an insect
escaping her hand.

"The wind's winning again,"
my Jewish grandmother says,
looking at a painting of Pushkin.

"Everyone in this house
will thank God for this profile."
Then she crosses her heart and

watches the storm begin
with pale green eyes
and hopes to die.

My mother dies in Wisconsin while I am excavating in Egypt

I turn off the noisy drill, the earth
hardly needs piercing after weeks of a
surgical sun. "It is only a matter of
discovery," our obscure physician writes.
My father writes it is natural
to be so ill. I come quick as a child,

her room is musty green. (Another of her
Egyptian stories, the world blossoming
with ugly things and queens) Her lips
swell like Cleopatra's when the pretty
thing was over. (My father pushes the
tongue gently back again) I am told

I may kiss her but she does not
kiss me back. (For God's sake seal her up,
I've had enough) The undertaker hammers down
the nails. My hands feel the wood like a
cryptic inscription. The coffin sinks
into my skull, the diggers work hard

in the hot ruins. I pay them well
for showing me something
I had not known: her death
is the tunnel to
the deepest remains. The doctor
sews up my skull with chilly fingers.

On Jumping off the Queen Elizabeth in Summer

Foamy wreaths rise to fill the hole.
The wind cocks the waves, "for-death" signs
glisten like trophies, piles of sun raised
from the deep trespass are untouched.

The need to close the nose, o vexatious
undertaking! The water airtight, the flesh
easily scraped, the light light, the fluid
mothering. I nurse at the blue nipples of

anemones, drift down through yellow woods
to a muddy shack below. My father is asleep,
he doesn't care that first night, sleeps
in the recesses of my mother's breasts.

Morning, like propellers, swings around
through the air, the sawing grows frantic,
travelweary, the blades bewildered. Memories,
on edge, fall on the sharp chant of wounds.

Morning. The Queen puts my soul off at Halifax.
The captain's first cup of coffee slices the
clouds. He has left me forty miles at sea, lying
against the warm side of mud, a great sea butterfly

waiting for lungs and eyes.

To Watch It Snow

It's snowing, my daughter
has just spilled some tea.
I scold her but hug
her body between my legs.

She slobbers and points
to the center of her kitty's
nose. We are not friends.
I put on her smock and try

to get her to write from
left to right. Like a drunk
she suddenly loses interest
and very seriously drags her

chair down the hall to the
window, folds her arms and
is content to watch it snow
from right to left.

From the Beginning

I was telling her on the phone
about the rape in the next town.
Why did I need to frighten her
before lunch? I felt marooned on
rings from one call to another.

The grass is heaped around our house.
Our little girl lies in the hammock
of her arms. She is a clear, measured,
robust, touching life. If either dies,
I will prefer the other dead too.

On Sunday night, after our girl is asleep,
we go to see *The Virgin Spring*
in the next town. Dark carpets
are nailed to the shiny floor. Gray
paint is heaped on the seats.
When the film comes, I fly my hand
over my wife's thigh, comforting her.

My Parents, My Life

Memory is a wave on a wide river,
masts swaying on the dark water.
Stones stand out, in the distance
bodies float, water roaring in
their mouths. I am afraid to go
too far. Far off, a man staggers
along a swamp, grasping reeds. I

turn, sweaty and old like my father
whose eyes shine when he turns too
abruptly. The sun climbs the middle
sky and hangs there quivering. Drunken
uncles and aunts collapse on cots,
snoring in a week of green flies and
flashes of lightning in July. It rains,
flies swarm up, sting my daughter's

arms but she protects them. It is out-
rageous that she is here. I had dreamed
of a boy. In the smoky room my parents
lie wrapped like people who no longer
need air. My wife struggles with our girl.
If I could, I would tell them they
are a silent movie I saw years ago.

In the background, I am my father, the
first to say sad is sad, eyes are eyes,
see the flaking crosses beside the river.
We shall paint them again this year,
rise and walk arm in arm through
the wild vine of sun. All week following
the visit, I keep smelling my father
clean fish and my mother cook

for relatives, their hearts restored to
see others eat. My mother removes her
scarf of black flowers. It is my sign
to recite Pushkin. Never in my life
have I hated anything so much as those
lines she loves. Her arms hang in the
vapor of the room. My fists tremble,

I reach out but lose my father
in a grassy river where barges
drag and pass. My mother sees him
too, but says nothing. I try to
outshout all the silence
in the world. I am dead and
I am shouting, a reed growing
from my swamp heart.

V

It's
me
who
hears
the
fountains

Century after Century

From the rain water
seeping through soil
to the deep rocks, wives
no longer become mothers,
except by dreaming.

Snow follows snow, steering
toward cities, dreaming
of men on river banks
who will save it from drowning,
unexpected fathers undressing
to do miracles at last moments.

To the Statue of an Egyptian Queen in Rome

(freely after Albin Zollinger)

Italian noon,
the height of time. It's me
who hears the fountains. I
wait and wait the tourist hours,
a lover returning to love.

Your hand is
an epitaph on your small girl body.
You sleep the gnarled sleep
of petrified trees. Your hair
flows in the wind of my mind,

precious
to your slaves, who sang when the Nile
rose in the leafy Ethiopian morning,
their tears a landscape
in your eyes.

Now the
grass on your head is thin.
Red gods, I stand loving. I come
the dusty summers to see your face stand still, a dial
whose styles project the sun of an ancient childhood.

On a Tunisian holiday, I study Arabic, drink
seventy-one bucks of fig brandy and make it with
my wife occasionally in a damp bed, the
radiator on medium

It's like striking the solid flesh
of the eucalyptus tree, instructing
the leaves to go wheeling, bowed
but thirsty, a tide of roots in
the brain. The sky is empty and
correct, like a famous city.

The old Arab who owns the place
strolls in front of our window
while we do it and writes magic signs
on beetle backs. He's still there
in the morning, a beautiful person
by birth. Perhaps our son will

be like him, equipped for weather
of all elements. O to see a son now,
the hostility of no teeth, to come
for the first time on a powerful
nose, to strike his mouth with

a gift, to speak the fucking
language. All we can do is wash up
and hope, straddling the silly sink,
imperatively quiet, we who have
been intimate in Tunisia, two
middle-aged Americans not far

from Carthage, from the broken
graves of Roman children. The
headstones are giant beetles,
caught upright by the sea taking
them to itself. The sky tries
the same with the moon and sun.

In the Mind's Eye

Shakespeare would see the sex of women
hanging in the wings of slender terns.
Besides his outside eyes, he had
another in the center of his brain.

For interior shores. Modern science
is startled: in the center of our head
a cone is evolving like the third eye
thrusting through the lizard's crown.

Hamlet did not sleep in the room
with his sword. (The room of dreams is sharp)
The plain of his eyes, lying like a shield,
turns the swollen world towards the sky.

The Auction

The auctioneer demands
we live up to the past.

For a quarter we get
a bent American Flag.

On the stairs, a woman's
college diploma goes.

The grandfather clock
is accustomed to its interior.

In the attic, my wife
gives a dime for a pewter spoon.

I use an abandoned flag pole
to walk the tightrope home.

My wife licks at the pewter.
I carry our baby eagle upstairs

wrapped in the flag, accustomed
to rising with little air.

Ballad of a Chinese Painter

(after Albin Zollinger)

I paint a lake
and a wooden bridge.
A dwarf moves
through my snow.

I paint a mountain,
a cabin in a valley,
a lamp in the cabin.
The dwarf moves closer.

I paint some snow,
steeply up a volcano.
Land like a moon.
Poor dwarf.

In the light,
his wife bathes another.
So he goes on,
erring like snow.

Clouds smother the sky.
Now the snow
becomes a lake,
and gently he enters.

When I was young
I thought I dreamt
what I painted.

But now the tea swirls in the waiting bowl.
Mountain after mountain,
dwarves in valleys, darkness of lakes.

Flying the Hypotenuse

Birds draw arcs
across the sun
with the compass
of their instincts.

Pythagoras saw the set
of such geometry, lying
in his skull on the grass,
figuring out

the coming caravans
chasing bees from their tents.
He and they are only dream
so we on the move this morning

are rare but still
must walk with two legs
while the bees and birds
fly the hypotenuse.

Dead Cat

(after Albin Zollinger)

She lived
in forests of sleep.
Which moon struck rays
in the strange branches
of her eyes?

Now she lies,
the wide split still in her legs
which did not carry her over.

Arborescent,
like the unicorn
in the bottomless arid landscape
of our eyes.

The Owl and the Pussy Cat

Every time I read it Sarah gets me high
on questions and God toward the end of
the lake and a spruce in the middle. I
can't get around it for all my pretending.

Tonight, deciding to try again, I discover
her sudden opposition. She hangs the owl
and the pussy in her brain. I hold them
up to my eyes, revived, but never see God
from whom they're suspended. In this bright
sudden summer night they fade from the pea
green boat and Sarah won't even play the owl's
guitar anymore. It is her worst depression.

Seeing eleven stars still above is not enough.
Lying in the lake on rings of pea and green,
I try loving Sarah and the owl and the cat
but drown somewhere off the rafts of light.

July 12

Milk runs from udders.
Rye rises yellow and I
swim toward the summer.

Stork shadows fall from
the white chimney. The
smell of sun in sawdust
startles the girl scout
pedaling by.

The green foams up
before the hills
baroque with love.

I sail toward myself,
crippled by the shadow of
the day on the year.

VI

The
Middle-West
Mystery

Dreaming of Floods

for David Young

The river, broad and
black with rain, swept
trees out of the way.

He felt a longing for tea,
the exhaustion
of a Chekhovian man.

For an instant
the early morning light
was green. Men in dark boots

sandbagging the water
were too late. He would
gladly have gone back to sleep.

There was a need to get up,
to drive several miles out of town, simply
to die.

Parents pressed like earth into the corners
of the storm window. I sketch them with coal
on the best paper I can afford. The tornado
left the house a few feet off the ground, the
southwest corner intact as the warning promised.

The bridge replaced the ferry across the Ohio
near Toledo in 1929, so Mom and Dad could have made
it across to the duke's palace or the military barracks
or the church, buildings typical of any post-reformation

period. And what their Bible said about menstruation
is true. Hence the survival of blood and forests. The
protein in the mountains clusters at the foot. And
the trees have disappeared from every tree street

in America. Follow the roots down through the bed
of gray lovers, lifting each other's corresponding
stone. Next time the wind will investigate the north-
east corner of such a house, the area of landing,

the roofless air, the minimum height. Diagonal saw-
cuts split my parents' block. From the dressed surface
a hole issues round water and I assume the excrement is
dried up deep inside. Outside now, the water is a

trench of relief. A part of my mother's dress hangs
oddly down, her breasts hardly indicate the folds. But
I can tell her by the descent of the calves to the
ankles, a surviving dedication to a Babylonian deity

whose feet did not show. The dried veins all
around parallel obscurity. The same figure
of a father will be found much later by a son
in a recessed panel of wind and confirmation.

Shallow and Deep

Balloons of light
circle the shallow
morning. The reeds
around my feet bruise
the heads of the garter
snakes. I cut several
wagon loads of cedar
and raise the flag
on my land today. It
is hard on the wrists.

In the deep afternoon
I start back for the
farmhouse. My wife is
inside watching me melt
to water before the sun.
(Therefore here is my body)

Her vision
cannot cross the bridge
I was cutting down today.

November

Sometimes the winter's fires
leave black spaces
in the stubble of my heart.
They grow one by one
into the green of grass,
as secluded as the menstrual moon
draped with folds of thin white cloud.

It is the other moon's turn,
clear and white as noon, reading
the shadows of the woods.

Something so November in this
forces me to walk cross
the field just covering
its seed black. The earth
flows in rigid currents
around my settled brain.

Source

Water shows between the patches
of steaming weeds. Birches reach out
branches so low I crouch to guide
my bait to the brown trout guiding
his weight toward the steep darkness.

Falling ducks move with gravity.
How does a fish find balance in
his hooked flight? I follow him
to shore, an odd place for a man

of black grass marshes and no sense
of change. On each side of the rope
of water, we lie toward morning,
furrowing the sand, waiting, mingling

with each other's reflection, returning
the light to its source, darker than
marshes, dark with a great darkness,
broken only by breakers from
the breathing of a heavy sleeper.

My Life Is Insane

I kiss it in the hospital garden.
It is all in white. It
smiles at the grass or a bench.
We walk together to the bridge,
then it runs with all its might
toward the open field.

All afternoon I hunt it
but only find some
beetles fallen on their backs.

The Gift

Birds sitting on the burnished roof.
An open window on poplars juggling the sun.
A little water in a little glass by the bed.

He thought it important that death should come
in this familiar guise. Sunrise, smell of
ripe grass, birds stitching. He envied her

the end of her illness. She was no more
the vague girl he had married. He came closer
but she gave a warning touch, pulled

some needles from a basket and
began knitting some mittens
for her cold hands.

Last Visit

She sat in the high-ceilinged room
among tubs of rubber trees. The river
was dark with ducks crossing the sky.
It is not death for gliding bones.

Suddenly she moved and I followed,
rocked in the cradle of the wind.
In an hour, we reached the orchard
on the far side of the sanitorium.

She looked everywhere at once
like the goldeneyes in the
crowns of the trees. Caught
in a red web of apples and sun,

I called promise you'll come back
for our game. But she did not hear.
I turned around relieved. I knew
I would fill with absence.

My Dear Rosemary

Like most lay people I know
little or nothing about
death. On the surface it
was classically medical,
the last white corpuscles
lodged between the cancer
and your stained breasts.

But on the whole it was
chaotic and created the
impression of a crisis
of authority. Perhaps a
husband does not stand
sufficient distance from
the superior facial quality
of a New Testament wife.

The priest was persuasive
and instructive and yes
memorable, he spoke with
a minimum of introduction
and hardly any notes at all,
letting you speak directly
and that changed my attitude
toward the Church. The coffin

is wider than I thought
it might be, I am amazed at
its horizontality. I help
close the earth and depend
on a narrow stone, a quarry
of limited sermons. Now my
hands put flowers on your
grave. If only they would
stick to their regular habits.

I Die

The family on chairs
are bored.
They cannot tell
where the sky is.
Their hands
tap several times
on the oilcloth, talking
so well I keep silent.
Outside, my kids
on the lawn
dry like linen.
A red dog browses.
The moon rises on its back,
like my memory of myself.

I look up, dry-eyed, see
my headstone. I am
convinced I was a good man.
"Here lies" is a lie.
The priest passes, his
glasses glisten so much
I give up. At the cemetery
gate my wife rushes ahead,
airier than a shadow. She
fears I shall follow her
like worms. Is she afraid?
Quickly.

Old Graves

I draw the bolt across the door,
douse the lamp, open a shutter
and fire into the dog's bark. I
feel in my pocket for the last
bullet, drop it gently to bed.

The lamp in my brain
shines on the hammer, the
hammer strikes the chamber, the
bead bounces from tree to rock
to field to me. Gradually, gradually

I think of death and die for
that flying bullet. It is then
that the hills are baroque
with old graves falling
below the level of soil.